NO MORE PICKY EATER

For Kids

WRITTEN AND ILLUSTRATED BY *Esther Smith*

ISBN 978-1-59433-622-5
eBook ISBN 978-1-59433-623-2

Library of Congress Catalog Card Number:
2016930423

Book designed by Esther Smith

Text and Illustrations Copyright 2016
by Esther Smith
—First Edition—

All rights reserved, including the right
of reproduction in any form, or by
any mechanical or electronic means
including photocopying or recording, or by
any information storage or retrieval system,
in whole or in part in any form, and in any
case notwithout the written permission
of the author and publisher.

Publication Consultants
http://www.publicationconsultants.com

NO More Picky Eater

Written and Illustrated by Esther Smith

This book is dedicated to my little girl, "Ninni Bug" (that's what her brother calls her). Many of my children have gone through food therapy to learn to eat and handle the textures of foods. But in rural Alaska, we are not close enough to any large town that enables us to receive such services. So, for her turn - it's mommy's job to teach her. There are many people who are not in an area where they can receive help. So, this book is also dedicated to you and your children who need this kind of assistance. "Thank you for your support!"

I am often tired and feel grumpy and "cranky".
My Mom and dad say that part of this, is because
I am a "Picky Eater".
They say that I feel "cranky" because
I don't eat enough food...
and the food I do eat, isn't good for me.

I only like ice cream, crackers, doughnuts, and milk. In fact, I don't really like to eat at all. so, I usually only eat about 3-7 crackers, one doughnut (if my mom gets me one), and 3 cups of milk...for the whole day. Mom and dad say that this is not healthy

But I know some other kids, who eat only one or two of their favorite foods, unless their parents won't let them. Even then, they scream and fight with their parents, and usually win, and get the food that they want.

Adam likes only Apples and apple juice.
Bradley likes only Bananas and orange juice.
Cathy likes only cookies, and eats a lot of them.
Dustin won't eat anything but doughnuts.

What about you?
Do you only like only one
or two things too?
Maybe your favorite is:

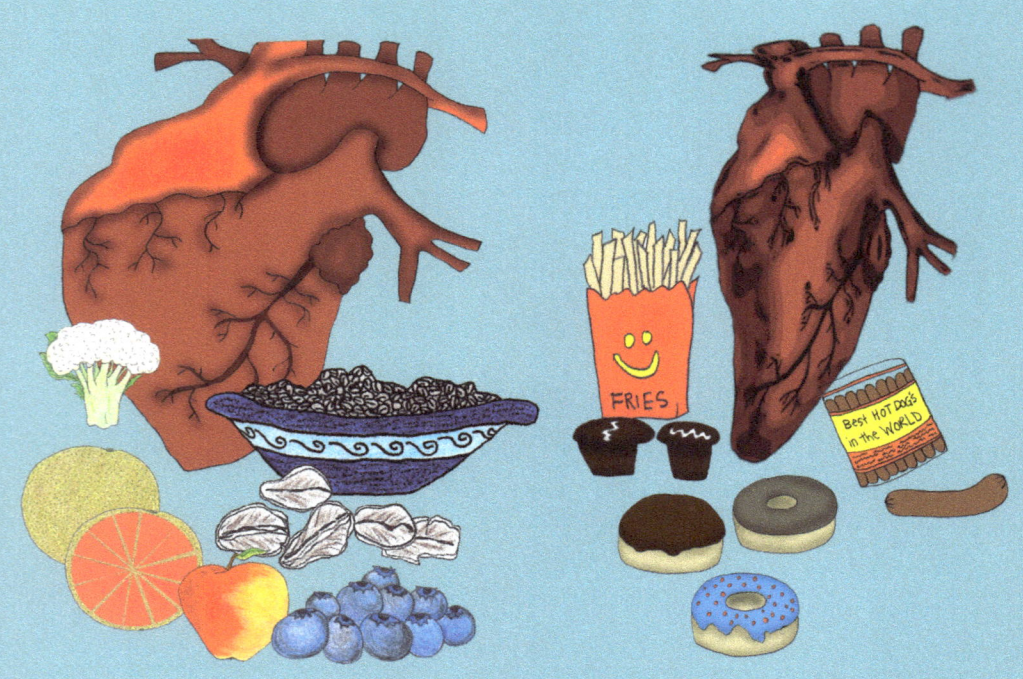

We will get sick, because the different parts
of our bodies need to have the right type of
food for them. For example
there are foods that feed our heart
and foods that if we eat too much of,
are bad for our heart and they hurt it.

Here are some of the different parts of our body that need to be fed:

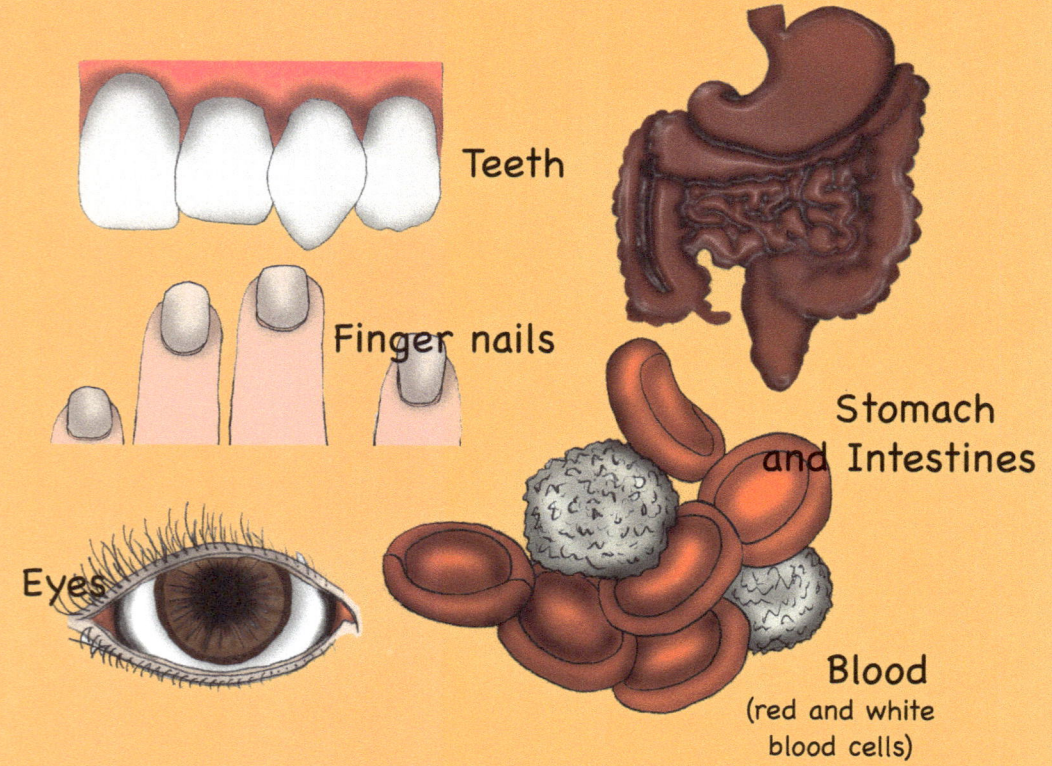

Teeth

Finger nails

Stomach and Intestines

Eyes

Blood (red and white blood cells)

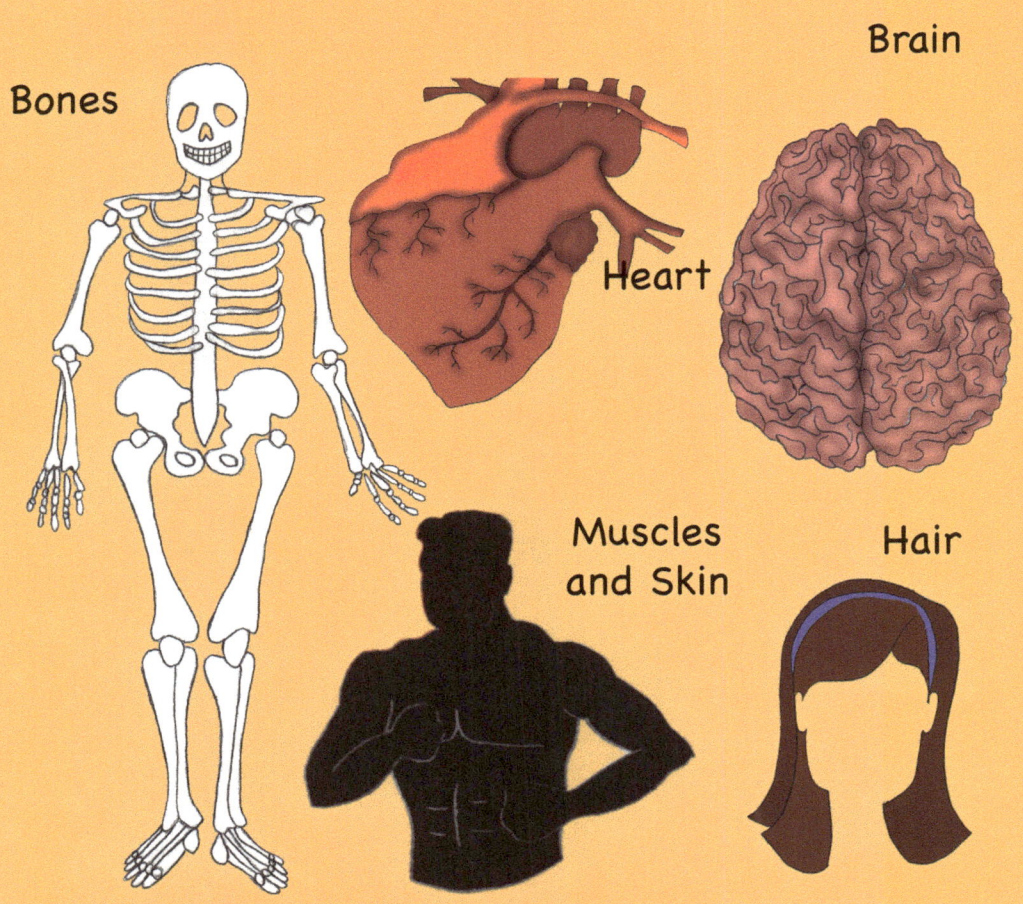

Here are some of the foods that are good for them:

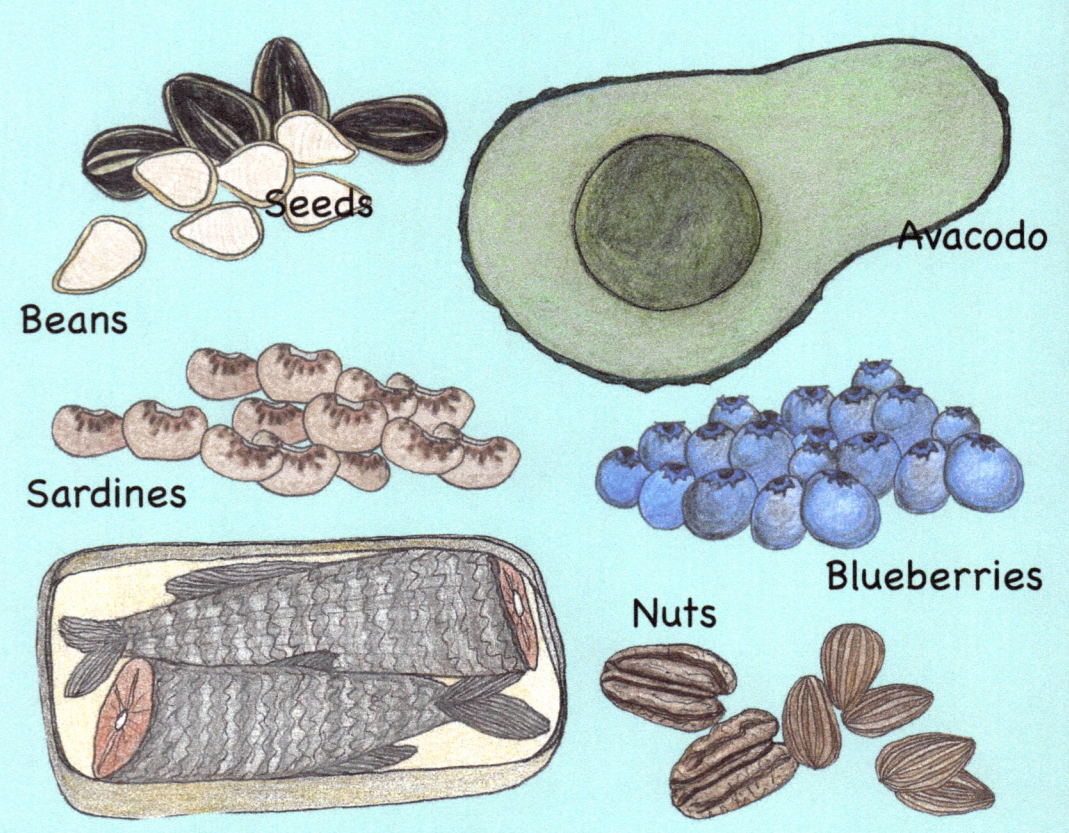

If you only eat food that is good for your eyes,
and never eat anything that is
good for the rest of your body...
than the rest of your body will be
very weak and hungry.

But if you never eat anything good for your eyes...then you could go blind.

If you never eat anything that is food for your brain, then your brain cannot think very well, and you will not become very smart.

We all want to be smart so we need to pick at least one thing that we can get used to, from the foods that are healthy for our brain, and practice eating it.

We wouldn't want to eat only brain foods though, because our brain would get really smart, but then our muscles wouldn't be able to get us around to go to school, play, or do anything – because they need food too.

That way each part of our body is getting fed an equal amount of food and will grow evenly, and none of our body will starve, or be too big.

There are also foods that are very bad for us, they hurt our bodies. Some of these foods can hurt us quickly and others may take longer to hurt us, but are still very bad for us... especially if that is all that we eat.

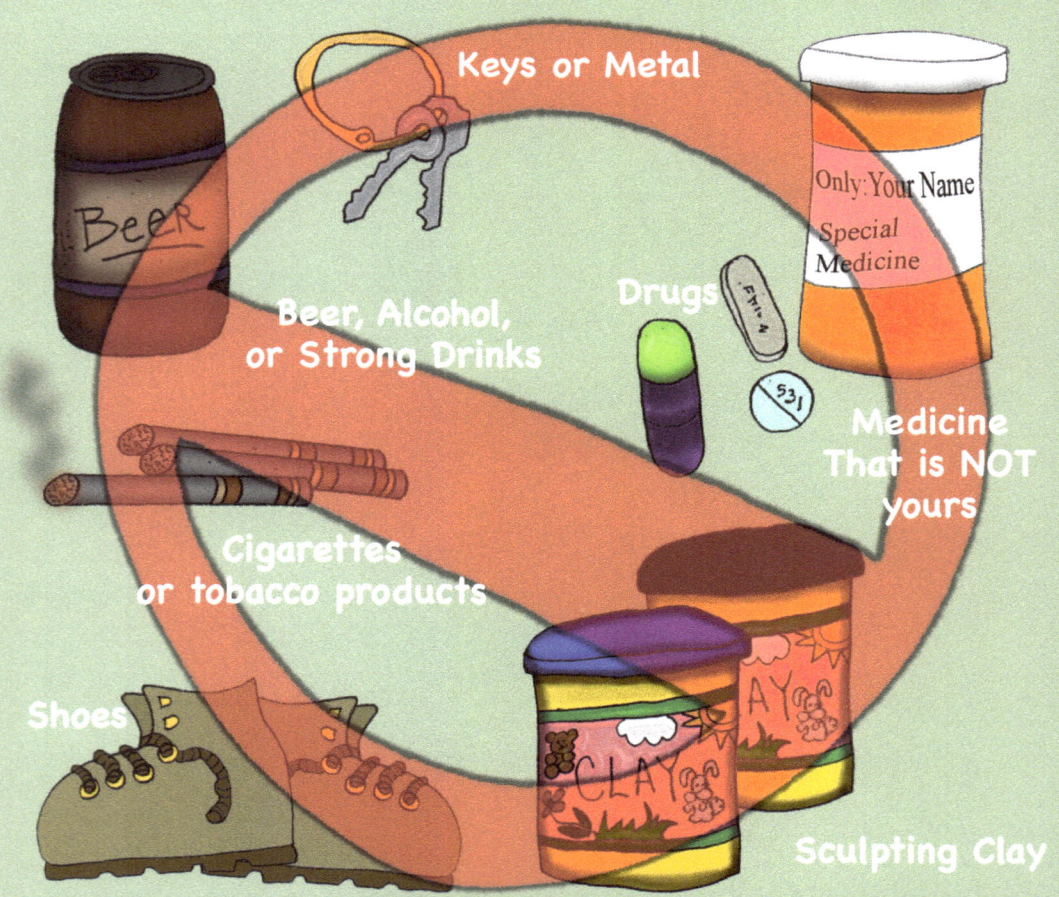

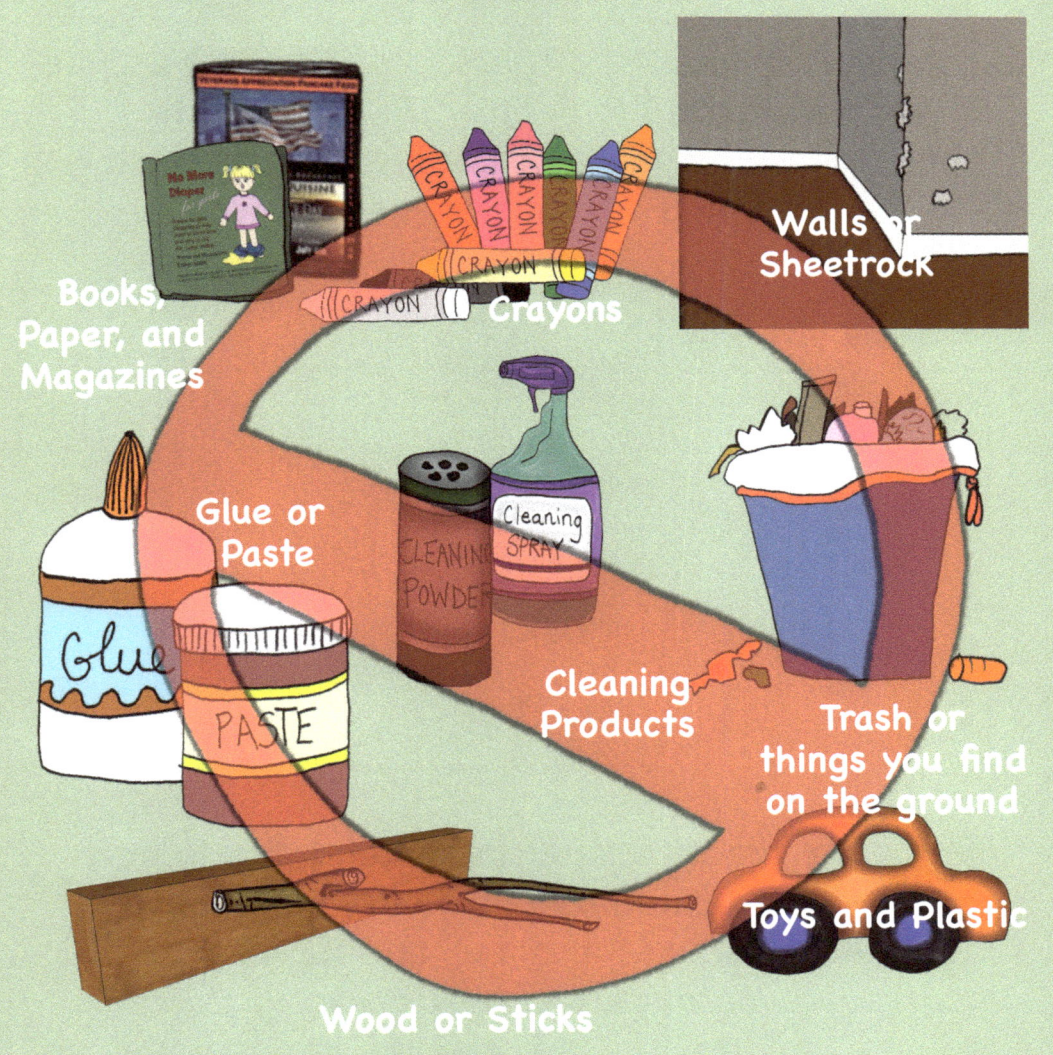

Sometimes a food might look scary to us because we never tried it before. Or maybe it has some bumps or pokes or dangly things hanging off of it, and that makes us feel weird.

But if we practice being brave and trying new things, we can help our bodies be happy, feel better, get smarter, and be able to do more and play more.

Here are some ways that we can learn to get used to new foods:
Try just touching a new food.
Poke it a little, play with it a little till you get used to it and it doesn't freak you out any more.

Try smelling the food,
taking breaks in between,
but try smelling the food
three or four times,
before deciding it is not for you.

Now try touching the food to your face.
Touch the food to your cheeks,
to your chin, and to your lips.

Eventually touch the food to your tongue.
You still don't HAVE to eat it yet.
Now try to let it sit on your tongue.
Hold it there for a second.
Try closing your lips around it if you can
(at any time you can spit it out if you need to).

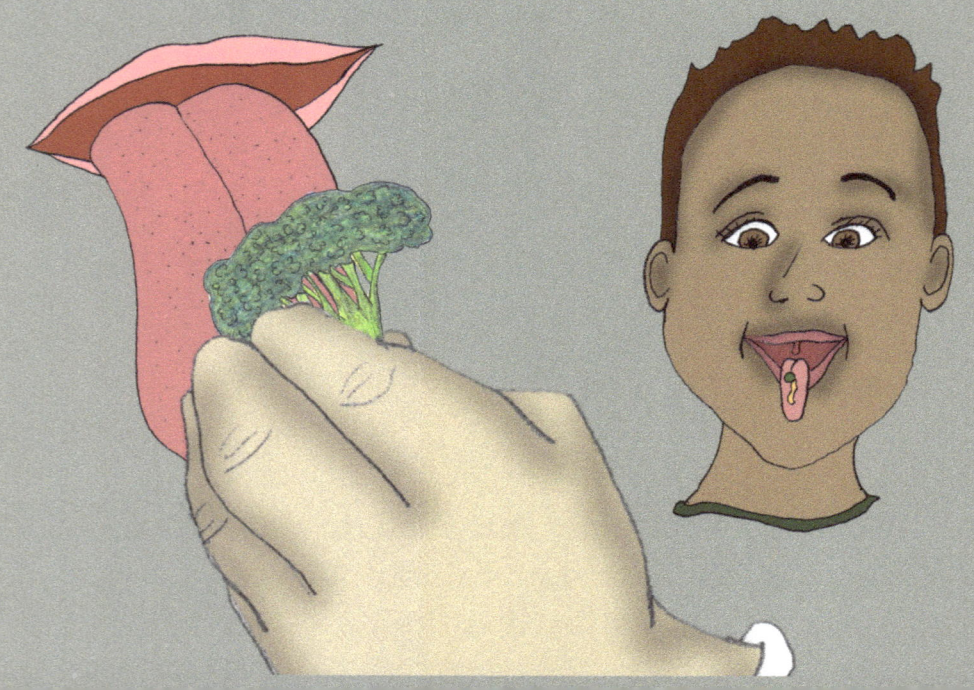

Let your tongue touch it over and over.
Pull it out a few times if you have to and
are still too afraid to close your mouth
around it. Let your tongue get used to the
bumps, wiggles, and pokes that may be
happening in your food. Now swish the food
from side to side, letting the inside of your
cheeks feel the new food. You are doing
a great job when you get this far.

Now try taking a bite of the food.
Chew and chew and chew it.
Chew it 10 times...if you still can't stand it,
spit it out into a napkin, the trash can,
or wherever your parents recommend.

But...if you are really brave,
you will take a gulp and swallow it and see if
your belly likes it. You will never know if
your belly, brain, heart, or body like it,
if you won't swallow. So, go ahead and try it out.
One new food at a time.

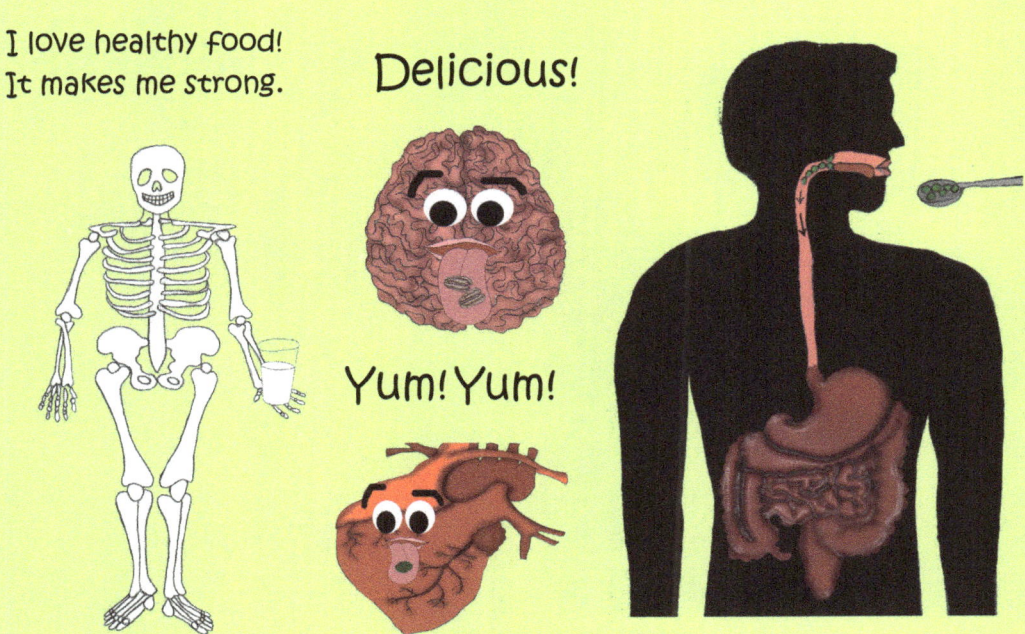

If we find something on our plate that we are afraid of, or really do NOT want to try, but somebody gave it to us... the best thing to do is to leave it alone!

It can't crawl. walk, or move next to your other food. It just makes us feel like we are supposed to eat it. Well, we don't have to...but we should try some new food, as often as we can.

Don't scream about it, cry, freak out, take it off your plate, complain, or say, "Yuck!"
Just pretend you can't see it and leave it alone.

My parents told me all of this, and I've been trying it. I like a lot of new things now, that I never would have known – if I only stuck with what I already liked. Now, I even like some things that are mixed together. I never thought that that would happen, but now that I tried them... I really enjoy them.

I ♥ U Food!

I hope that the rest of you will try this out too and find out for yourself how many wonderful, delicious flavors there are out there...and though you may not like some most are awesome!
You'll never know, if you won't try it.

No more picky eater!

No more cranky me!

 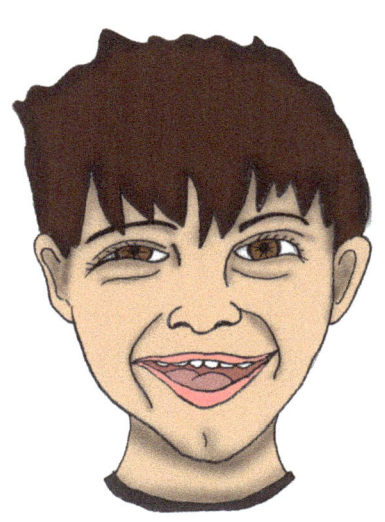

TIPS FOR GETTING YOUR CHILD TO EAT

Try to give your child something you know they'll eat (that won't fill them up, and is healthy) first thing in the morning...for example some low-sugar yogurt. Then offer them a couple of new choices that are colorful, but healthy, like an apple or orange if they don't regularly eat these. Get them excited about it. This will help get their stomach juices going.

Eat with them. Also, eat the same things you are offering them. Kids aren't stupid... if you offer them an orange, oatmeal and yogurt and tell them, "these are healthy and yummy", and then you have a Poptart, soda, coffee and doughnuts - or you drive through at fast food, they won't believe you. Nor will they want to eat what you offer them. Actions speak louder than words. Kids and all people follow examples, a lot better than dictators, and if they see you having healthy eating habits and sitting down at regular times with them to eat healthy things, they will follow your lead.

Avoid caffeine, sugar, and any other stimulants ever for children...these things are not healthy for anyone, but they fill people up with useless carbohydrates that spike your sugar level quickly - making people, and especially kids, very hyper and restless. Then very shortly afterword, they will feel starving again and will want more "junk food" not whatever healthy thing you have to offer, because these additives are habit forming, addictive, and leave you empty with a lot of health problems later in life (including, but not limited to: Diabetes, Obesity, Irritable Bowel Syndrome, and more).

Don't wait too long between meals. Often if one waits too long before eating a healthy snack, or meal - than their body thinks it is going to starve...so it overcompensates for the lack of food, goes into starvation mode, and dumps a bunch of sugar stores. This is not a healthy thing and does not make you loose weight. It is very bad on your organs including your pancreas, liver and kidneys. However, you or your child will suddenly feel full or at least not very hungry. Then they'll avoid eating a healthy balanced meal. They may crave sugar and be willing to eat "junk food", but too full for actual real foods. Later the body will realize it is actually starving again, and you or your child will be tempted to overeat. Not only will they wish to overeat, but they will desire "fast acting sugars" such as orange juice, candy, and they will get into a vicious and unhealthy eating cycle.

If you have waited too long to eat and your child gets grumpy, starts freaking our, hitting, screaming, sweating, etc., they may need some fast acting sugars, because their blood-sugar-level may have dropped and they may even pass out or fall asleep if they don't get food right away. Should this happen, do not use "white sugars" or highly processed foods to help them (unless they have childhood diabetes and you've been told otherwise by their doctor)...instead, first use orange juice, honey, peanut butter with jam, or something that doesn't take forever to digest, but isn't so unhealthy or filling as candy and junk food. Next try and get them to eat something solid and healthy.

Reward your child with the foods that are their favorite. Don't give them those first, or they have nothing to work for. Offer to your child that if they first pick something healthy (give them a few choices - not too many - kids get overwhelmed and can't pick), then they eat that item, then you will give them another healthy item they like. If they don't like anything healthy, they may have a tiny portion of some type of treat; but try to do that very sparingly. For example, if your child likes bananas...offer him/her some pecans, rice, peas, or green beans. Let them know that if they eat one or more of those things, that they may have a banana. If a banana is not enough bribing for them to try a pecan for the first time, maybe offer them 3-5 small candies out of a bag, not the whole package. But only offer the treats if they will not try the healthy foods. Healthy foods can be rewarding on their own, once people get used to them.

Allow your child to play with their food if they are learning to eat it for the first time. If they already like the food and are just making a mess to be a stinker, you don't need to allow them to play with that specific food. However, many food therapists have suggested that one of the best ways to get a kid to be willing to put a new thing in their mouth, is to let them play with it first. It makes sense why often toys go in their mouth more than food. So, even though it may just make you cringe to allow them to finger through their rice or spaghetti...it really is a natural process that if they are denied as a cute little toddler, they will have to work through later when they can throw a lot further and make a much bigger mess, or they will never learn to eat a wide variety of foods.

Play with your child while he/she is learning to eat, too. Help him/her play with their food in a more structured manner. For example, zoom a spoon of peas into their mouth while pretending it is an airplane or a choo-choo train. Pretend that a potato wedge is going for a dive into a condiment and now it is swimming into an underwater cave (their mouth), or other creative ideas.

www.ingramcontent.com/pod-product-compliance
Lightning Source LLC
Chambersburg PA
CBHW040323050426
42453CB00017B/2439

9781594336225